Teaching Purity in an Unpure World

Teaching Purity in an Unpure World

...with no experience necessary!

RANDAL LEE

Table of Contents

Introduction

Parenting – it's not for the faint-hearted.

You've braved 2 a.m. feedings, ear infections, teething, projectile vomiting, and more ungodly diaper disasters than you care to count. You've proven your stamina by lugging around twenty pounds of baby wipes, Desitin cream, and jars of Gerber's strained peaches in that diaper bag permanently affixed to your shoulder. You've navigated the rocky terrain of potty training and those infamous terrible twos – all while fielding what felt like a million curious questions, like, *"Daddy, why do dogs have tails?"* or *"Mommy, why does the moon look orange sometimes?"*

It's a challenge, no doubt – but how special is it to know that your toddler cherishes your insight and comes to you for life's little answers? Hopefully, that never changes.

However, as they grow older, their questions become far more graphic. Some are easy to tackle, while others leave you speechless. But no question will catch you off guard quite like the dreaded: "What about sex?"

While you're still scraping your jaw off the dining room floor, your teenager sits there, eagerly awaiting your great words of wisdom. The pressure is on. Frantically, you reach deep inside, scrambling for the right response – only to come up empty-handed. So, you blurt out the easy answer: "Uh…that's for marriage!"

Then, as the lump in your throat finally subsides, a nagging thought lingers:
Was that enough?
If you're wondering whether that answer was sufficient – maybe. But probably not.

Hold on – don't panic – this might help.
The book in your hands could revolutionize your efforts and make that jaw-dropping moment a lot easier to swallow. Through practical suggestions and a common-sense approach, the author draws from his own past struggles and lessons learned, offering a path toward redemption

and wisdom for his child. It certainly won't do the talking for you, but it can equip you with the confidence to face even the toughest questions head-on.

This world presents unique challenges for this generation – and your children stand in the crosshairs, awaiting your reply.

I know you want to give them the best – and this book can help you do just that.

Chapter

1

Two Lives Collide

He was barely twenty. She had just turned eighteen. Naive in many ways – yes – but they were certain of one thing: this was more than just infatuation. What they felt ran deeper. The very thought of life together was all-consuming. With starry eyes and heads in the clouds, they mapped out their future – plans they believed held bright promise.

It was an exhilarating time for two zealous young hearts. Unfortunately, neither had the faintest clue what they were getting into – or the countless twists and turns that lay ahead: the hardships, the struggles, the harsh realities that would test their love. So, throwing caution to the wind, they eagerly bought their tickets, jumped in, and held on tight.

The ride would be wilder than they ever imagined.

The Weight of the Past

They carried scars – wounds from promiscuity, heartache, failed relationships, broken families, even sexual abuse. All of it came into the mix. Baggage that would weigh on their marriage for years, forcing them to confront painful memories they had long tried to forget.

How would all of this shape their future?
Would their marriage last?
Would their love withstand the weight of their past?

Only time would tell.

His Story: A Reckless Youth

For him, the struggles began in adolescence – a headstrong boy with too much freedom and too little guidance. He was determined to test every boundary, convinced that "If it feels good, do it." His parents assumed he was acting on his best behavior, never questioning his choices or observing his activities. It wasn't that they didn't care – actually, they cared a great deal. They simply didn't notice. Ultimately, he was left to his own devices.

Assumptions can be dangerous. Like the summer he and his neighborhood friend built a wooden fort in the backyard. They sketched out a plan on a Big Chief Writing Tablet, then raided his dad's garage for nails, boards, and concrete mix. To any outsider, it was just a harmless project – two boys hammering away at something that looked like adventure. But behind those crude walls, where no adult ever checked, curiosity took root.

That's where it happened.

In the shadows of their secret fortress, with no supervision and no guidance, he had his first sexual experience – with a neighborhood girl who had been invited inside. No one suspected, No one asked questions. But something had been awakened that day – a spark that would grow into an unquenchable flame.

In his home, the subject of sex was taboo. Aside from the quick, dismissive demand, "Just don't do it," he couldn't recall a single meaningful conversation about it. There was one awkward lecture from a church youth leader, but the focus was more on restraint than on the beauty of what God created. What he took away from that message was simple: *God is out to spoil my fun.* No one gave him a compelling reason to wait.

The people who really needed to step up – his parents – never truly did. They made a few attempts, but they were half-hearted at best. Besides, they were dealing with problems of their own. His father, consumed by extreme anger, filled their home with turmoil. Violence ransacked his childhood, leaving him feeling helpless and out of control. In an attempt to cope, he turned to sex – through the lens of pornography.

With no guidance, he navigated this dangerous territory alone. He indulged in his mind, and at times, in his body. To him, sex became the ultimate gratification – the ultimate comfort food, so to speak. And pornography? It seemed harmless…at first. But what started as innocent curiosity quickly tightened its grip, becoming a full-blown addiction. Years later, he understood the truth:

The damage ran deep.

Experts say it can take seven to ten years to heal the emotional wounds inflicted by pornography. He could attest to that. His choices had consequences – ones that haunted him well into adulthood.

The result?
Baggage. And plenty of it.

Her Story: A Broken Home

Her struggles were different – and just as painful. In fact, even greater.

Divorce fractured her family early on, leaving behind confusion and longing. And her story only grew more complicated. The fifth of six children – five girls and one boy – she desperately needed a strong father figure. But the one man who could have made all the difference was absent. Though she has since built a relationship with her real father over the years, he wasn't there when she needed him the most. Caught in a legal battle, he stepped aside, believing it was for the best. Unfortunately, his choice caused him to be alienated from his children, rarely visiting during their formative years – a decision he would ultimately regret. His absence left a void no one else could fill.

Her mother did her best to compensate, working tirelessly to provide for her children. To her credit, she not only worked hard, but also went above and beyond. She made every occasion – Christmas, birthdays and special moments – feel meaningful and memorable. She also possessed the unique knack of squeezing a dollar till it gasped for air.

But when it came to guiding her children through the moral dilemmas of those tender years, she struggled. In her search for stability – and for the father figure her children so desperately needed – she made some extremely unwise choices. The numerous men she brought into their home were often abusive and manipulative – some even incestuous. These men were far from honorable. With Mom constantly working to make ends meet, the children were frequently left to fend for themselves. And without a stable father figure, chaos ensued.

As a young girl, she watched her home life unravel. She saw her siblings' promiscuity – some of it ending in pregnancy. She witnessed her mother's multiple failed attempts at marriage and learned a blueprint for infidelity – one that was destined to fail.

By the time she was a teenager, she had seen more than her fair share of dysfunction, as the world around her reeked of instability. And, when the particular man – who claimed to love her mother – turned his attention toward her, she learned the painful truth:

Love was not what she thought it was.

It was hard enough to be without her actual father. But to be forced to live with a stepfather who said he loved her – yet took advantage of her – was even harder. For years she battled the hurt of that abuse. God's grace eventually allowed her to forgive the man who selfishly violated her, because he wasn't her actual flesh and blood. But forgiving her mother for allowing it to happen? That was a whole different story. She struggled with that for decades.

She, too, was left to figure things out on her own. But one thing she knew without hesitation – she didn't want to follow in her mother's footsteps.

Deep down, she knew her mother loved her. But she needed more. She needed to feel safe and protected – and she needed her father. Lacking that, she went searching for love and acceptance elsewhere. Confused about what love really meant, she followed the only blueprint she had ever known – and set out to find a man who would fill the aching void inside.

Like so many teenage girls, she fell prey to the false promises of an insincere boyfriend. When he said, "I love you," she believed him. She thought his motives were pure. But once her innocence was gone – so was he.

The examples of promiscuity and unwed pregnancies she witnessed as a child led her down the same path – one that ended in an unplanned, out-of-wedlock pregnancy of her own. Now, alone with a precious baby in tow, she was determined to build a solid family life.

But how could she possibly succeed…when she had no idea what that even looked like?

Her story?
Even more baggage.

Chapter

2

No Big Deal

Baggage – there's that word again.

How much can two people carry before they break?

It was the one thing they really didn't need, but they couldn't escape it. They could only imagine what it would have been like to be truly innocent on their honeymoon night. He recalled a conversation he'd had years earlier with a so-called friend:

"Wedding nights can be so awkward when you don't know what you're doing, so isn't it better to be practiced up?" his friend smugly taunted. "Everyone should have a little experience under their belt, or they'll never know what good sex really is. After all, you do want to perform it right, don't you?"

Then came the next thought: *Do I honestly need a 10-step program to learn the skills of lovemaking?*

He knew full well that having so much so-called *skill* wasn't all it was cracked up to be. In fact, promiscuity was like a dog darting from one experience to another. *I don't think there's any great talent in that,* he thought.

Even if his wedding night had turned out to be a complete awkward disaster, they would have had a whole lifetime to learn together. The real challenge – the real genius – was to satisfy and be satisfied by the same person for a lifetime. And they longed for a marriage like that.

A Cost They Never Expected

They agonized over the thought, *I wish things had been different for us.*

Some say dredging up past mistakes is no way to live your life. But what do you do when the failures come back to haunt you all on their own?

There's something about the mystery of the unknown that's almost magical. Maybe it's the fact that as you grow closer in your relationship, you know you've only begun to discover the depths of intimacy that await you. Or maybe it's just the idea that there's something you haven't shared with any other person. I don't know exactly what it is – all I know is that it's something far more special than these two ever imagined.

Regretfully, what should have been new and exciting now felt bittersweet – just another encounter. No innocent first touch. No enthusiastic discovery. No lover's first vulnerable embrace. Just ordinary – when it should have been extraordinary.

It's hard to describe the ache of knowing you've crossed a line you can never uncross. And it's not just about the physical – it's the sense of having given away something irreplaceable.

They had heard others say, "Everybody does it, It's no big deal."

But as they lay together, trying to embrace the intimacy that was supposed to feel natural and fulfilling, they realized the truth:

It was important. It was a very big deal.

The Invisible Wounds

Most married couples understand the tremendous connection that happens with sex. They also know the painful betrayal they would feel if that intimacy were ever shared with someone else. That's why adultery is so devastating – it's not just on the surface. It wounds the soul.

Most of the time, adultery remains unforgivable because – no matter how hard they try – the innocent party can't let go of the hurt.

But whether people realize it or not, that same connection begins even before marriage.

Sex is such a powerfully bonding experience that once you've been there, you don't easily walk away untouched. We are forever tied to our past by the invisible cords of our conscience. And throughout life, nature compels us to make comparisons with our experiences.

Sad to say, what happens within those bedroom walls is no exception.

They were learning that firsthand.

The past projected onto their present like an unwanted film reel, replaying every experience, every *someone*. Those mental intrusions hung like a shadow over their love life – for they knew they could have been the exclusive recipients of the pleasure their spouse provided. *Do you think that bringing all their 'knowledge' into the bedroom could ever compare to sharing that experience together for the very first time? How much more meaningful could it have been?*

I believe the true joy of sex is within God's design. It's the joy of indulging in each other with nothing to compare it to, nothing to critique it by. They agreed, *That's what we want for our marriage."* So they tried to bury those thoughts and move on with life – and it worked for a little while. But the amnesty for their actions was short-lived.

Ghosts, Demons & Pornography

While she dealt with ghosts of her past, he faced demons of his own. At first, he thought his struggles were the same – memories of past encounters replaying in his mind. But soon, he realized something more sinister had taken hold.

His mind wasn't just recalling real moments; it was haunted by something else entirely – the images of a long-standing pornography addiction that refused to fade.

Like salt on an open wound, those mental pictures – clear as yesterday – began flooding his thought-life. *Sure, I made mistakes. Hasn't everybody?* he reasoned. *After all, they seemed so harmless – even helpful.*

But he soon discovered that true intimacy and porn had nothing in common.

He wondered, *Will we ever reach a real connection? And if we can't – what then?*

Not only was it a stinging reminder of a moment in his life he would have preferred to forget, but it had penetrated the very area that should draw them the closest – their sex life.

He had assumed that marriage would erase his past struggles. But instead, it only magnified them.

An Instant Family & Growing Resentment

Starting life together would have been challenging enough with just the two of them, but adding a third – especially the all-consuming attention a toddler requires – turned the recipe into disaster.

He confessed, "Although I eventually grew to love my child, it didn't actually start off that way."

What kind of father looks at his child and feels resentment instead of joy? He couldn't believe he was even willing to say it out loud. But he continued, "The truth is, I wasn't just rejecting my child – I was mourning the loss of my own expectations."

Their marriage had problems from the beginning, making the first several years brutally rough – to the point where she thought, *Maybe I'd be better off if I simply packed up my child and left.*

She tearfully confronted her husband: "I feel like you're making me choose between you and my own daughter."

Quietly, he muttered, "She's always between us."

Deep inside, bitterness festered as he felt cheated out of time with his new bride. Jealousy was eating him alive. The weight of it was crushing – for they never had a moment to just be alone.

The gravity of the situation crashed over him like a tidal wave, and his immaturity only made it worse. The pressure of an instant family left him feeling trapped. Unprepared. Suffocated.

It nearly broke them.

By the end of their second year, the marriage was hanging by a thread – battered and barely holding on.

With no time to adjust, no space to simply be newlyweds, resentment grew. Anger became his downfall. He vented his frustrations on those closest to him. Yelling and screaming became the norm – but anger, left unchecked, rarely stays in words alone. His rage showed in mean-spirited, harsh behavior and slammed doors – sometimes coming dangerously close to violence.

And then – silence.

The kind that says more than words ever could.

Soon, his behavior became glaringly apparent to those on the outside. He could no longer function as if nothing were wrong. He admitted, "I know I need to change. I know I need help."

So, they prayed – and God answered.

It all began the night he kicked a hole in the living room wall. Shocked and afraid, she rushed to dial a church friend. The wisdom her friend shared that evening was this:

"God has you both on the operating table. You can lay there and allow Him to perform His work, or you can get up and call it quits".

They decided to stay and see it through.

They felt a nudge to move – away from the past, away from the naysayers, away from the voices telling them, *You'll never make it.* So they packed up and moved out of state – and God was waiting there to help them heal.

It wasn't just a change of address. It was a turning point in the story of their lives.

Sometimes, God calls us away not just from a place, but from a mindset, a pattern, a past that clings too tightly. Moving didn't erase the problems, but it gave them space to breath new air, to see each other differently, and to rebuild what had been torn down.

It was in the unfamiliar that they discovered the unexpected grace of God.

They say that time heals all wounds, but time alone wasn't enough.

He needed to grow up.
He needed time to work on his marriage without outside influences.
Time to bond with his family in a meaningful way.
Time to appreciate the precious child he was now responsible for – the child he once feared would be his demise.
His belief that a child could negatively affect his happiness wasn't just misguided – it was ridiculous. He needed to learn how to sincerely appreciate the family he had been entrusted with.

As if every event were divinely ordered, things slowly began to change. Behaviors shifted, and they grew as a family – not just in size (as they now numbered four), but in maturity as well. Church life became a regular rhythm, healthy friendships flourished, and time spent together turned into cherished moments.

He took a serious look at himself and his explosive anger – something passed down through the generations from his father – and said, *That needs to stop.*

But his outbursts were learned behavior, carried over from his childhood. He came to realize that his unchecked anger was actually a form of victimization – and causing his child to become a victim was a step too far.

He had to take hold of it… or risk passing it down to his children.

The church they were led to had an unwavering focus on family. I believe this was no mere coincidence. They got involved in marriage ministry and immersed themselves in becoming better parents.

As the years flew by, his heart softened even more. His thoughts drifted back to one particular day as he watched his little girl playing in the yard. As if God were speaking audibly, he heard a voice say:

"I will change the person you are… and I will do it through her."

And He did.

Chapter

3

Reshaping The Future

It's been 18 years since that fateful day we jumped on the rollercoaster ride of marriage – and we've never been happier.

However, we're not the typical story of a baggage-toting couple that gave up. Many others in our situation had already traveled the road of separation. But shortly after all the glitz and glitter of the wedding ceremony faded, we quickly realized one undeniable truth:

Marriage is hard work – period.

Even if we had started with a clean slate, it wouldn't have guaranteed smooth sailing. Marriage can prove to be a real challenge, and for many starry-eyed lovebirds, that alone is enough to knock them right off their perch. But when you bring heavy baggage into the equation, the odds of survival are stacked against you.

We knew deep down that something had to change – not just for us, but for the little ones watching. It wasn't just about healing our marriage; it was about breaking the cycle for good.

Facing Hypocrisy and Finding Purpose

We asked ourselves, *Who are we to tell our kids not to do what we had done ourselves?*

Besides, what would two people with our background have to say about proper behavior anyway? We already felt like failures in this area. Wouldn't that just make us hypocrites? But then it occurred to me – being a hypocrite means continuing to practice the behavior you condemn. And that wasn't the case at all. We had confessed our wrongs, changed our ways, and moved on with God.

So how could this be hypocrisy?

Everyone has failures in life they truly regret, but we couldn't allow that to stop us from giving advice on such an important issue. Besides, who better to warn them about the pitfalls than someone who has already suffered the consequences?

Just because our past came knocking didn't mean we had to invite it in for dinner.

A New Legacy Begins

You may be thinking, *This sounds like me.*

Just like us, you may have dreamed about opening your "gift" with that special person you were committed to for life. But reality proved to be a cruel teacher, and it mercilessly dashed your dream to pieces.

Instead, maybe you gave it away in the back seat of a car, a cheap hotel room, or the dingy basement of your parent's home. Wherever it was, it probably wasn't the shining moment you had hoped for.

Even if your past feels like a cloud of guilt hanging over your head, the good news is this:

Not all hope is lost.
There's light at the end of the tunnel.

Is failure knocking at your door? If so, I'm here to tell you:

You're still entitled to a Fresh Start.

You can't change what's already happened – but you can shape what's to come. In your hands lies the ability to reshape the future of your family, starting right now.

Here's a way you can do just that.

Building Strength for the Next Generation
Consider these two points to guide you on your way to generational change:

First, put to death the notion that you have no influence over your children. As a parent, you play a huge role in the decisions your children will make for their future. In fact, no one will leave a deeper or longer-lasting impression than you.

I challenge you not to leave sex education to a school – even if they are teaching an abstinence curriculum.

When statistics tell us that 39% of ninth-grade students are engaging in promiscuity, obviously their methods aren't working.[1]

Take ownership. Teach them. Talk openly. Be the example they can follow.

They need your input – and they are listening.

Secondly, stop believing that it's too late to change your situation.

One day, I was talking to a man about the ideas in this book, and he told me, "I think you're a day late and a dollar short."

Confused, I asked him, "What do you mean by that?"

Well," he said, shaking his head, "it's too late for me. And as for my kids, they're adults now – so what good is all this information?"

I spoke up with conviction, "How about sharing it with your grandson?"

---

[1] NIH MMWR Morbidity & Mortality Weekly Report - CDC

Suddenly, his face lit up as he realized the legacy he could leave behind. He walked away from that conversation ecstatic with the thought that he could turn failure into an opportunity for change.

The vision of his grandson possibly experiencing the clean start he never had – that was priceless.

Breaking the Cycle

From what I've seen time and again, behavior tends to repeat itself. The patterns we grow up with will keep showing up — unless we choose to stop them.

Like the man who felt it was too little, too late, you might wonder if change is even possible.
But hold on — this might just be your moment to turn things around.

As loving parents, we'd never intentionally lead our children toward harm. Yet even with the best intentions, it's easy to avoid the hard conversations. And when we do, we may leave them vulnerable without realizing it.

How can that be? you ask.
Please, read on.

Looking back on our own childhoods, my wife and I saw unhealthy patterns in both of our families — poor communication, an acceptance of promiscuity, and a failure to model marriage as sacred.

These weren't new problems. They were cycles that had quietly repeated for generations. If we didn't make changes, those same patterns would keep repeating in our children's lives too.

Someone had to break the cycle — for us, that moment came, and we chose to say yes.

Maybe you're feeling that same pull. It's not easy, but it's worth it. When we started, it felt like climbing a mountain we weren't ready for.

But every cycle ends with someone brave enough to break it.
That someone could be you.

And if you take the step, you'll be giving your family a gift they'll carry for life.

Chapter

4

The Gift

After experiencing the consequences of our own early struggles in marriage, I can't stress enough how important purity is – and how damaging the lack of it can be.

The challenge, however, is that teenagers need more than rules. They need a reason – something logical, something real – to wait. I was determined to give them one.

But how?

I couldn't simply tell them to follow my example, since my example wasn't worthy of being followed. I needed to provide something that would show the tangible benefits of purity and, at the same time, bring the idea to a level they could easily understand. I found that solution through a mixture of several diverse sources I'd encountered over the years.

Pleading, threatening, or guilt-tripping simply doesn't work with young people. More than anything, they need to see how purity can benefit their lives. In fact, demanding obedience is often the least effective approach. And even if they obeyed my demand, that's not what I wanted.

I wanted them to make their decision based on their own conviction – not simply because Mom and Dad said so.

I made it clear to them that although their choices would hurt us deeply, we wouldn't be the ones to pay the ultimate price. *They* would face the consequences.

In an age of instant gratification, I understand this can seem like an impossible task. *So* is there a way to make purity attainable?

I believe the answer lies within the pages of the Bible – five short but powerful verses in **1 Corinthians 13:4-8:**

Love is patient, love is kind. It does not envy, it does not boast, it is not proud. It is not rude, (or lacking self-control), it is not self-seeking, it is not easily angered, it keeps no record of wrongs. Love does not delight in evil but rejoices with the truth. It always protects, always trusts, always hopes, always perseveres. Love never fails.

With this Scripture as a foundation, I illustrated my point to my children through a practical demonstration. It proved effective. Of course, I adapted it for each situation; to avoid repetition, I'll share only the female version.

(see the male version in the addendum.)

The Night It All Changed

It was a Friday, one week before her thirteenth birthday, when I arranged a date night for just the two of us.

We went to a beautifully decorated, somewhat secluded restaurant nestled in the foothills of the city. It always offered a magnificent view, and when you looked out over the twinkling lights below, the scenery was simply breathtaking – a fine establishment for such a special occasion.

There, from our dimly lit booth by the huge bay windows, we gazed out across the city lights, exchanging the standard father-daughter small talk. Like most thirteen-year-old girls, she loved to talk – and talk – and talk! We chatted about everything from school to boys to the latest fashions – all the typical "young girl stuff." We joked and laughed as we shared an elegant meal together.

That evening, I tried to create an atmosphere as relaxed and comfortable as possible. Soaking it all in, I found myself enjoying every minute. Even to this day, we still recall just how special that night was for both of us.

As the evening progressed, our conversation turned to the real reason I had brought her to that place.

I looked into her eyes and said, "There's something very important I want to share with you." I reached into my coat pocket and retrieved a compact Bible I had hidden there earlier. Turning to **1 Corinthians 13**, I began to read: *"Love is patient, love is kind. It does not envy, it does not boast…"* and on and on I read as she listened closely.

By the look on her face, I could tell she was wondering why I brought her to a restaurant just to read the Bible to her. Then I said:

"The reason I read this Scripture is because I believe God is the author of true love. If you really want to know what love is, all you have to do is look to the Bible."

"Now that you're thirteen and growing up fast, I'm sure you're becoming more aware of the opposite sex – and that's only natural."
The subject clearly sparked her interest, and she leaned in a little closer to catch the whole story.

I continued, "But when you're ready to date, I want you to be alert and think clearly about the person you're with. First off, I really don't want you to say *'I love you'* to anyone you're dating until you understand what that truly means. And if he says to you, *'I love you'* and then starts pressuring you by pleading, *'If you really love me, you'll prove it to me,'* I want you to know how to handle that.

Always remember: "words are cheap.
But action?
Actions are the real proof of sincerity."

The Test
"The one way you can find out if he genuinely loves you is by doing this little test. For the sake of argument, let's

call this boy *Johnny*. Since Johnny says he loves you, use his name in place of the word *'love'* in 1 Corinthians 13."

"Ask yourself:
- Is *Johnny* patient with me, honoring my feelings?
- Is *Johnny* kind...respecting my desire to please God with my body?
- Does *Johnny* boast to his friends about what he's trying to get away with when we're alone?
- Is *Johnny* too proud to tell others that both of us are saving ourselves for marriage?
- Does *Johnny* have self-control in his actions toward me?
- Or does he struggle with his desire, rudely pressuring me for pleasure?
- Does *Johnny* seek his own satisfaction at any cost, or is he rejoicing in the truth of what God has designed and crafted for marriage?"

"Does *Johnny* pass this test of love? Because if he really loves you the way he says he does, then the proof of that love will be in his actions toward you."

The Illustration

I continued, "I know that someday you will meet the right young man, fall in love, and become his wife. But, until that time, God has given you an extremely precious gift – the gift of virginity."

At this point, I reached into my pocket and pulled out a small box of chocolates – the kind that has just four pieces in the package.

As I held the box, elegantly wrapped like a wedding present, I told her, "This represents your virginity. This gift can only be given once – and only to one person. God intended it to be given to your lifelong mate. Right now, it's a perfect and beautifully intact package with a bow on it – completely pure"

But let's say, one day, you decide to open this gift too soon. You find yourself attracted to a young man – let's call him *Charlie*. Your attraction leads you to be a little less careful than you should be, allowing emotion to take control – and you let him touch you. "

I then removed the bow from the package.

"Next, you meet another boy – *Bobby*. He seems to be relatively nice, but Bobby turns out to be the kind of guy who likes to push the limits. He pressures you to go beyond your comfort zone, and though you hesitate, you give in a little. Even though the gift is still unopened, you're feeling very guilty."

I then began to unwrap the box, tearing off the paper. "Since Bobby didn't get what he came for, he hits the road."

"Then *Chuck* walks into the picture. Chuck is a smooth talker. He charms you and continues to pressure you for proof of devotion. One night, the pressure becomes too much –"

I opened the box, pulled two pieces out, and placed them on the table.
"You surrender – and give your gift away. The next day you find, as abruptly as all the others disappeared, so did Chuck."

I know you think this could never happen to you – but it happens all the time. And when you look back at your gift of virginity, you'll realize all that remains to give to your husband will be this."

I showed her the torn, tattered, opened box with missing pieces.

Driving It Home

At that moment, I had her undivided attention.

With the next part of the illustration, I drove the point directly at her heart.

I reached into my pocket again and pulled out another identical, perfectly intact box. Holding both side by side, I said:

"People who look like this"– raising the tattered box – "often end up with people like this." Then, raising the intact one – "And people who look like this usually end up with someone who has also kept their gift intact."

"Now, picture your honeymoon night. Imagine the disappointment if your husband had saved his gift for you, but in impatience, you had already given yours away. Picture handing him this torn, empty box and saying, *'This is all I have to offer you.'*"

"Will he feel cheated? Will he feel the gift has been cheapened? Will he wonder, *'I saved myself for you…and this is what I get in return?'*"

"Do you really want to risk your future for a moment of pleasure? Please think about it and ask yourself: *'What do I want to give and what do I want to receive?'*"

By this time, tears were streaming down her face. I knew something deeply powerful had happened that evening. From that moment on, our relationship was never the same. It felt like we connected on a whole new level – and it has affected her behavior ever since.

She now carried a sense of purpose – a mission – and that mission was to marry in purity.

She told me, "When I walk down that aisle in a pure white gown, I want it to mean what it's supposed to mean – white is for virginity."

Making It Stick

Knowing that the typical attention span of a teenager is about 20 to 30 minutes, I wondered how to help her retain everything we had talked about.

I remembered a college professor once saying the best form of recall was a visual aid. That made sense to me. I knew it had to be something she could carry with her – a constant reminder of that night.

Since she was a girl, we decided on a ring. We chose a beautiful band designed with two gold hearts – one with her birthstone, the other with mine. As I held her hand, I told her:

"For now, this ring represents the idea that I am the man in your life."

Placing it on her left ring finger I said, "I pledge to be, to the best of my ability, all the character traits described in 1 Corinthians 13. I'll try my hardest to be patient, kind, long-suffering. I will do my best to be an example of the kind of husband you should one day be looking for – a husband with those same character traits."

(I didn't realize at the time how important this act would become later on.)

"But on the day the right young man comes along and asks for your hand in marriage, he will remove this ring, switch it to the other hand, and replace it with an engagement ring.

This symbolizes that he will be taking over where I leave off."

I can't count the number of times she has had to defend her decision to stay pure. Comments are a dime a dozen – and everyone seems to have one.

A particular remark comes to mind, and it went something like this:
"Don't you test-drive a car before buying it?"

I was so proud when I heard her response. Resounding with confidence, she shot back: *"Wouldn't you rather buy a new, unused car than an old clunker that's racked up high mileage?"*

Now that's what I call character.

Chapter

5

Paving The Way

We all want to see our children stand tall and resound with confidence when faced with moral pressure – but that kind of character doesn't just happen overnight.

You can talk until you're blue in the face, and still your words will go in one ear and straight out the other.

They're more impressed by daily actions.

In a book I read recently, I stumbled across a sentence that was so simple and yet so profound. It said:

"The battle is not won or lost with one statement."

I believe what the author meant was this: If you expect one little "talk" to instantly solve the problem you're having, you'll probably be very disappointed.

Just telling them, *"Don't do that"* (like my parents' advice to me) probably won't cut it with most kids today. You need to be consistently building a relationship with your children for your words to ever have a true impact – and it's within that context that you earn the right to be heard.

For your youth, the path of puberty will be littered with potholes. The rough road of sexual confusion and uncertainty will surely take its toll, and they'll be looking for some answers.

Where will they go to find them?

It's at that moment that your relationship will determine whether they can come to you for those answers – or if they need to search somewhere else.

Just remember: you are the one who will create the atmosphere where they can feel comfortable enough to ask.

Learning from Experience

I'll let you know that we've never been perfect parents. We've tried our best and gotten a few things right – but we've also failed miserably on occasion.

It's from the vantage point of those mistakes, made early on with our two teens, (now 16 and 19), that I can share a few secrets we've learned along the way.

The important questions will most likely be posed to the person with the strongest influence in their lives – and that should be you.

The following ideas are not rocket-science...they're just simple keys that will enable you to unlock the doors of respect, clear the lines of communication, and help you gain the influence that is so desperately needed.

Connection

One morning, as I drove down the I- 25 corridor on my way to work, a bumper sticker on the car ahead of me caught my eye. It read:

"Be good to your children. They'll choose your nursing home." I chuckled to myself and proceeded on my way, but for some reason, the words on that sticker stuck in my head. I asked myself, *"What was it about that statement that caught my attention?"*

About an hour or two later, it hit me. As humorous as that sentiment is, there's a seriously powerful truth behind it:

If I expect my children to respond positively to me, then I need to respond to them the same way.

In other words, if I really want them to listen and take my advice seriously, I must first build a healthy connection. I realized right then and there that's what I wanted most of all – a good healthy rapport. I had never experienced one with my own parents, and as a result, I was never able to truly connect with them.

It's obvious that a bad connection is often the result of poor communication.

"But how are parents supposed to connect with their child?"

If you've spent any time watching television talk shows – not that I'm advocating them – you'll see the problem: so many parents are trying to become their child's best friend.

Your place is not to become their buddy, and that's definitely not what I meant by rapport.

What they don't need is a partner in crime – they need a parent.

But there's a big difference between a parent who just goes through the motions and one who's truly plugged into their child's life.

Those who will see the most profound success are the ones who utilize the "bonding moments" that present themselves throughout everyday life.

I saw one of those moments just the other day when I was involved in a fender-bender with a young lady – probably not much more than seventeen. Unluckily for her, the fault of the accident was undeniably hers. I could tell she was visibly shaken as she dialed home to inform her father. In the meantime, as we waited for him to arrive, we surveyed the damage.

Roughly 20 minutes later, he stormed onto the scene to assess the situation. I watched carefully to see how he would response to his daughter's obvious distress, and what I witnessed was nothing short of disgraceful.

There was clearly pain and remorse in the huge tears streaming down her swollen face, but I never once saw her father try to console her. He didn't hold her or even try to calm her fears. In fact, he spent most of his time talking to me and apologizing for what his daughter did to my car.

For this clueless father, right here was an opportunity of a lifetime – and he missed it..

Am I saying something good could have come from this accident? As far as the car was concerned, not necessarily. But emotionally? He certainly could have secured his bond with his daughter. He had every right to be upset – but the remorse she showed should have been enough to gain his empathy. Yet it wasn't.

A tender hug or maybe a kind word – something like *"Everything's going to be all right"* – would have been appropriate. But greeting her with that cold, callous demeanor only cemented her suspicion:

She would never be able to approach him with more important matters – like sex.

She would remember that day far longer than he would. And I'm sure, from that point forward, her dad became much less influential in her eyes.

A lack of influence is also a direct result of poor connection – or in other words, bad rapport.

But on the other hand, little acts of compassion and understanding can strengthen your impact with a young person. If they see that you're willing to deal compassionately with them in other areas, then when they're faced with moral issues, you'll be the first person they turn to.

And that's exactly what you want.

But many times, we fail to make that connection, and unfortunately, we lose our influence.

When I read the passage where Jesus said of John the Baptist, *"There was no one greater born of a woman, (Luke 7: 27-28)* "I was curious to know what traits Jesus considered so great?"

Among several others was the fact that John "came to turn the hearts of the fathers to their children." *(Luke 1:17)* I ask you, fathers: *"Is your heart turned toward your child – or does it need some re-adjusting?"*

I know it's easy to feel as if our only obligation is to take care of the necessities – to provide shelter, clothe them, feed them, and do whatever else it takes to keep our family afloat.

But as for their emotional needs? *"I'll leave that up to their mother to deal with."*

Again, I ask: *If Jesus held fatherhood in such high esteem, shouldn't we?*

Have you let this world dictate to you what a father should be like?

The gift of raising children is serious business – and it's an honor that I accept passionately. How about you?

Life is more than the pursuit of worldly possessions. It's a pursuit for the heart of your child. And you'll capture his or her affection when you're involved and genuinely interested in their lives.

Sometimes they feel like they're standing on the shoreline of life all alone, and they need someone on their side. Be the one who bridges that distance – by finding ways to gain their trust and influence. Those opportunities happen every single day.

"A gentle response defuses anger, but a sharp tongue kindles a temper-fire." – Proverbs 15:1 ™

Cherish

It's not just how we respond to our children – it's also how we respond to our spouse that determines the strength of our influence.

Once you've crossed the chasm and joined your child on their side of the bridge, the next thing you need to realize is: *Your children are watching you… intently.*

So, the question becomes: *"What are they seeing?"*

This truth never hit harder than the day I met Bryan, a college acquaintance from a small university I attended years ago. He struck me as someone who had it all together – a loving wife, two wonderful boys, and what appeared to be a great relationship between the four of them.

On more than one occasion, I spotted him and his wife at school functions, married couples' events, and even strolling hand in hand across the well-manicured campus. When he spoke about his sweetheart, he always used kind words. He seemed to treat her with honor and genuine love.

As far as I could tell, he had the perfect marriage – and I assumed it had always been that way.

But I was about to learn differently.

One day, as we casually chatted after class, our conversation shifted to marriage.
I told him, "I admire the relationship you have with your family, and I want the same for myself."

He smiled, but then replied, "Don't be too impressed with me, I haven't always been a wonderful spouse."

With a shadow of shame in his eyes, he confessed that early in his marriage, he nearly destroyed his wife – and his children.

"For some reason," he admitted, "I started to belittle her… and I don't even know why. It began with little things, like calling her 'my old lady' and 'the ball and chain.' But it didn't stop there. Soon, I was making tactless remarks – even telling her to 'shut up' – sometimes in public"

She was utterly humiliated. These comments weren't just made in front of strangers, but in the presence of family and friends as well.

Eventually, a close friend noticed the behavior and confronted him.

"That was enough to stop me from treating her that way in public," he admitted. "But the problem didn't go away – it just moved behind closed doors."

In the privacy of their home, he continued to demoralize her. As a result, she grew increasingly bitter and distant. Bryan thought everything was fine because he was saving face in public, but he was blind to the fact that his children were watching everything.

They heard and saw it all – his hurtful words, her bitter attitude, and how his actions devalued their entire marriage.

I'm not sure that anything could have inflicted more damage on those two boys than the way he was treating their mother.

After all, this was more than just his wife – this was their mom.

What his two sons witnessed caused them to resent their dad deeply, and little by little, his marriage began to crumble.

That continued until one day, after verbally bashing his wife one more time, he told me, "I turned to see my oldest son watching me with tears in his eyes."

Those drops of pain penetrated Bryan's calloused heart, and for the first time, he saw the hurt he was inflicting on his family.

His spirit broke.

Suddenly he understood, and in a voice dripping with regret, he said, "What I had been able to hide from the world, I could never hide from my children. They read me like a book!"

If your child were asked what they think about marriage, would they say, *"I want what my parents have"* Or would they see something completely contrary to the vows you made at the altar?

The way you live your life when no one else is around speaks volumes. Your kids know when your marriage is cherished as a gift – and when it's merely endured like a prison sentence.

They need to see you snuggling on the couch or sneaking a kiss in the kitchen. They may act like it's gross, but deep down, they want to witness a healthy relationship in action.

Show them you enjoy each other's company – and that you hold marriage as a top priority.

Your children will either embrace marriage or reject it, based on what they see in your relationship.

If you show them that your marriage is precious to you, they'll want what you have – and they'll be willing to wait for it.

Let your relationship become a goal for them to strive toward.

If you do, there's a good chance they'll rise to the challenge.

Control

Before you "turn off" at the word *control,* hear me out.

At first glance, you may be taken aback by this word, but it's not as shocking as it may appear. I'm not advocating harsh strictness or extreme sheltering (that usually has the opposite effect), but I *am* talking about controlling the situations that lead to trouble.

The idea is not to "cut them off from the world," but to help them recognize the pitfalls – and avoid them.

We have a mandate given to us by the Lord: to *"point your children in the right direction"*
(Proverbs 22:6) ™ and part of that mandate is helping them chart their course in life. I think King David said it best:

"Come, ye children, hearken unto me...depart from evil, and do good; seek peace, and pursue it" (Psalm 34:11- 14) ^KJV

In other words, he was directing them to turn away from the situations that would create trouble in their lives.

The Bible is bursting with examples of those who instructed their children in making right decisions. People like Abraham

(Gen. 18:19), David *(2 Kings 2:1-4)*, and Zechariah *(Luke 1:62-80)* all chose to guide their children in life. If you choose to do the same, you'll be in very good company.

However, as a father of two, I know the next statement is contrary to every teenager's belief system:
Trust is not an inherent right.

Too much trust has gotten too many people into too much trouble.

As an adolescent, I was allowed an abundance of freedom with very little restriction – and that eventually paved the way for a lot of experimentation.
The truth is, most errors in judgment happen when young people have too much free time on their hands.

For example:
That extra hour between dinner and the movie…
Three unsupervised hours in the basement with no chaperone…
Time alone together behind a closed bedroom door…
All are potential disasters waiting to happen.

Don't be naïve.

It's easy to underestimate the importance of boundaries – especially with young people.

I know, because I've made that mistake myself.

Sometimes we unwittingly give our children that very opportunity to fail by not monitoring their activities.

I have always believed that trust is something they must earn through maturity. And showing maturity means proving they can be trusted in *every* area.

For example:
- Can we be confident that when they say they're going to a friend's house, they actually went?
- When they say, "Yes I finished my homework," did they really finish it?

Little acts of trustworthiness are what you should be looking for.

Although I personally felt sixteen was the earliest appropriate age for dating, I chose not to set a firm age limit.

It appears to me that when a strict age limit is set, it's like saying, *"Once you reach this age, you can do whatever you want."*

Instead, we wanted them to realize that as they showed responsible behavior, we would slowly relinquish some of our parental control – granting them greater freedoms.

In this way, we could allow dating when we felt confident that they were truly trustworthy.

Although, not with just anyone they saw fit – *we* would also need to be comfortable with their potential date.

Did *we* also feel they were responsible and trustworthy?

Some relationships are a collision waiting to happen – like the one I heard about more than 20 years ago.

This experience left a lasting impression on me. It reminded me how easily parents can be fooled when they trust without accountability – and how dangerous that can be.

It was just the beginning of another exhausting day on the warehouse stock crew. Work began at 4 a.m., but we would always arrive a little early on Mondays to drink coffee before jumping in. As usual, the stories began to fly within minutes of settling down at the table.

That break-room banter was usually interesting, but this day was one that would shock me for a long time to come.

I had worked with this young man for eight years, and even though his character had some serious flaws, lying wasn't one of them. In fact, I had never known him to exaggerate.

He started bragging about how he was seeing a preacher's daughter – and what had happened with her the night before.

He said her parents wouldn't allow her to date anyone who didn't attend church. In theory, this sounded like a good idea. But after hearing this guy's story, I wasn't so sure.

So, to appease their one simple prerequisite, he began attending services regularly. Over the course of several months, he gained the trust of her parents – and on that night, even went to the altar for prayer.

After the services concluded, he drove home with her family to spend time with their daughter.

Since he had been attending faithfully, her parents felt confident enough to allow them time alone — just the two of them, in a back room of the house. Settled comfortably in the living room, they had no reason to suspect anything was wrong.

But what they failed to see was that, on that very night, this young man was crossing boundaries with their daughter.

You can be sure those two youths were fully taking advantage of the unsupervised time they'd been given, while Mom and Dad remained completely unaware.

Parents, this is exactly why you cannot afford to step back too soon.

Staying engaged in your children's lives is not meddling — it's wisdom.

Like my pastor often says, *"It's not what you expect, it's what you inspect."*

No matter how much you trust them – or how well you think you've prepared them – life will throw unexpected curve balls their way.

There will always come a moment when you have to release them.

But if you haven't laid a firm foundation…

If you haven't instilled convictions that anchor them to purity…

You may well find yourself dealing with painful consequences.

Because sooner or later, most kids will test the boundaries you've set.

And when they do — when temptation knocks at the door — they need more than just good intentions.

They need clear principles and the strength to stand by them.

They need something solid to fall back on – a framework for wise decision-making.

On several occasions, we've been accused of sheltering our children so much that they were never given a chance to fail.

But that's simply not true – and in the next chapter, you'll see why.

Chapter

6

Kids Will Be Kids

I always assumed – or at least hoped – that my children would never do the things I'd heard other kids doing. I am sure you feel the same way about yours. But before you apply the final polish to their halo, consider this story. With my daughter's full approval, I share the following:

The Gift in Action

At age seventeen, we trusted our daughter and allowed her to go on a date without a chaperone. Even though she knew how important it was to avoid compromising situations, she ignored our warning – and did just that.

When her date asked her to go with him to a remote location to "stare at the stars" for a while, she went – against her better judgment. There, she found herself alone in a car with a boy intent on manipulating her emotions for his own selfish desire. Before she had ever agreed to go out with him, she had made it abundantly clear that she was a virgin and deeply committed to staying that way. Clearly, he wasn't as committed to that principle as she was.

He made his move, inching forward and attempting to touch her inappropriately. Even though she knew it was wrong, she didn't immediately "slam on the brakes." At that vulnerable moment, he leaned over and whispered in her ear:

"I know we both want to remain virgins, but I really love you, so won't you let me?"

Confiding in me after the fact, my daughter said:

"In that moment of pressure, I glanced down at the ring on my finger, and the first thing that entered my mind was *1 Corinthians 13: Love is patient, love is kind, love is not self-seeking ...*" Everything we had talked about on the night of my thirteenth birthday came flooding back – the test of love, the unwrapped gift, and the picture of what I wanted my first time to be like.

And it certainly wasn't in the backseat of a car.

"I'm not willing to settle for second best."

"I want the innocent honeymoon you spoke of – and I'm going to wait for it."

That simple illustration, replaying in her mind, kept her from making the biggest mistake of her life. Because she could measure real love by what the Bible says, she saw his true colors and told him:

"We're not going there. We're going home!"

I can't help but wonder: how many parents pray their child will remember their words of wisdom in a moment of crisis? And yet, how few prepare their child with something concrete to cling to?

That night, the ring was more than jewelry – it was an anchor. Because when temptation whispers in their ear, they won't have time to flip through a book – they'll need something immediate to hold onto.

Building Upon That Gift

In the previous chapter, I mentioned how our kids need a framework for the choices they'll face in life. So I ask: *What kind of moral framework have you built for your child?*

What will jolt them back to reality when nature starts to take its course?

Did you give them a simple pat answer – or a logical, sensible reason to wait?

Even though our intentions may be good, sometimes we're guilty of building a solid structure in one area but failing in others.

Have you heaped onto them a generous pile of financial savvy… but only a few crumbs of moral character?

I'm not opposed to education or financial security – both are important. But you also need to create in them moral conviction strong enough to withstand an onslaught of compromise.

If there's one thing in this life they'll come face-to-face with, it's *compromise.*

Neither my wife nor I were ever given a solid understanding or a vivid picture of what was truly at stake when we indulged our physical emotions. As a result, we had never been taught a reason to guard ourselves.

But the stakes were far higher than we ever understood at that age.

Someone once told me, *"You can afford to make a few mistakes in life – but when it comes to marriage, the price is too high."*

That's exactly where you want your kids to succeed – because a successful union depends on the right choices.

Keeping That Gift in Check

Sex has the uncanny ability to justify behavior and slap blinders over the obvious.

Solomon understood the danger of becoming physically attached when he said, *"Catch for us… the little foxes…that ruin the vineyards." (Song of Solomon 2:15)*

I believe those *little foxes* represent the subtle flaws and character gaps that can sabotage a couple's future.

It's in the courtship stage of a relationship when focus ought to be at a premium – so that flaws and shortcomings (those "little foxes") can be clearly recognized and then dealt with seriously.

But once sex enters the picture, it takes center-stage. Suddenly, facing potential problems becomes less important than the next moment of physical pleasure.

Thankfully, God has given us some insight into our children that can help us guide them toward the altar with 20/20 vision.

In *Psalm 127: 3* KJV it says,
"Children …are arrows…"
Why didn't God say they were a rock – something you could just throw over the years of puberty and hope they land safely on the other side?

Because, unlike a rock that's easily picked up from the creek bed, an arrow is not simply discovered. It is purposefully designed.

God has entrusted you with a "lump of flesh" – your child – to mold and shape with purpose.

He created them to be affected by you, and just as an arrow has three components, there are three areas of your child's life you should be working on.

The first is the shaft – the stick to which all the other stuff is stuck. The shaft is your child's **character**.

If the shaft – their character – is even slightly bent, everything else will be off-center.
You must build character before anything else.

In addition to the shaft, an arrow has two other components: the **point** and the **fletching** (or feathers).

The point is the part that directly impacts its target. The point represents their **personality**.

Personality is a good thing to have, especially if it drives them to pursue a goal. But personality alone will only get them so far.

It's like the story of a girl named Tina, whose dream was to win a beauty pageant title. Her personality drove her to pursue that dream with a passion. She wouldn't settle for anything less.

But on her way to becoming a major contender, she became infatuated with a boy. She started dating him and, as one thing led to another, she eventually ended up pregnant – forcing her to drop out of competition.

What Tina had in personality, she lacked in **wisdom** – the fletching that could've kept her on course.

The fletching is **wisdom**, and it's what balances the arrow so it can fly straight and hit the target it's intended for.

The larger the point (personality), the larger the fletching (wisdom) needs to be.

How will your child be expected to hit their mark if they're left to figure out sex for themselves?

Do you think their peers will have the right answers?
Do you think they will learn purity on the street?

It is your **God-given responsibility** to supply them with
the pattern to follow – and make marriage something
desirable.

You are the one who has the ability to **sharpen, shape,**
and **aim** them at the target.

Gather those arrows in your hand, draw back the bow,
take aim –
and hit a bullseye for your family!

*"Don't excite love, don't stir it up, until the time is ripe – and
you're ready."*
(Song of Solomon 8:4) ™

Chapter

7

Welcome To Payday

He was just twenty, and she was barely nineteen – but calling it *infatuation* would be putting it lightly.

With wedding bells already ringing in their heads, and the promise of a bright future ahead, every day was starting to look more and more like **our** story.

Only this time… with a clean slate.

To us, they seemed a little naive about the details – but then again, so were we.

It was just a matter of time before they, too, would take that huge leap...and hold on tight.

But the one thing they would never have in common with us was the pile of baggage hanging over their heads.

They would never have to be rudely smacked into reality by shame and regret.

Never have to experience the pain of a bittersweet honeymoon…

Or a critiqued sexual experience…

Or a tormented thought-life.

They'd never have to stumble over all of those things that had been so flippantly dismissed as *"no big deal."*

So, on **March 7, 2002**, our little girl got married.

That white wedding dress meant everything it was supposed to –

And for the frosting on the cake, she chose a man who was also **deserving** of the white he wore.

Ever since we first heard Wayne Watson's song, *"Somewhere in the World,"* we'd prayed for the young man who would one day become our daughter's husband.

If you've never heard this song, it's about a father praying for his child's future spouse – even as that child is growing up *somewhere in the world.*

It was on a brisk evening in October when that young man showed up at our front door for dinner. I'm not sure I was truly prepared for the moment he asked permission to date my little girl.

Or, two months later, when we all sat around the kitchen table and they both began talking about their intentions – that someday, he would ask for my daughter's hand in marriage.

I'm sure tension filled the room as I grilled them with a barrage of questions.

Looking back, I'd like to share a few meaningful moments that followed those discussions around the dinner table.

When he learned of the story behind the ring on his fiancée's finger – and the illustration that had been shared with her – he decided to show his appreciation symbolically.

On **Christmas Eve** of that year, we exchanged presents together, and one of the gifts he gave to me was a little box of chocolates – just like the box I used five years earlier.

Attached to the box was a note thanking me for sharing that illustration with his future wife and expressing how he looked forward to passing that message on to his own children one day.

That gesture meant the world to us.

It was truly refreshing to know that our daughter had found someone who would share with our grandkids the very values we had worked so hard to instill.

He earned our affection even more by taking his appreciation one step further.

On the night of his proposal, he wanted us there – **unannounced** to our daughter.

He was planning to pop the question in front of their entire youth group, and he had a special surprise in mind.

Earlier in the day, we met together, and he asked if I would hold the ring for him and bring it with me that evening.

As he sat my daughter down on a stool and bent down on one knee, we were brought in behind her – completely out of view.

With her unaware that we were even present, he had me walk over, remove the ring from her finger (the one I had given her on her thirteenth birthday), and place it on the other hand.

Then, pulling the engagement band from my pocket, I handed it to her soon-to-be husband.

I'm not sure there was a dry eye in the house.
As our eyes met, we shared a lifetime of conversation without uttering a single word.
I can't tell you how honored I felt for my son-in-law to include us in such a powerful way.
 And in that moment, I realized just how deeply we had impacted our daughter's life.

She had always told us she was looking for someone with the same character traits as her father.

And as you can imagine, I was extremely grateful that I had been able to model the kind of man she would one day choose.

I'm the last person to toot my own horn, so I'll tell you now:

If I hadn't asked for divine help – I surely would have failed.

But since we had cherished our own marriage…

Because we had opened the doors of honest conversation…

Because we taught her to question false promises…

She not only listened – she wanted what we had.

And when it came along, she was able to **recognize it**.

The Mad Rush

After an eighteen-month engagement, their moment had finally arrived – and the clamor erupted early.

Other than the excitement being slightly diminished by a lack of sleep the night before, our house had never been more alive.

In a frenzied rush, each of us grabbed a "to-do list" and hit the streets running. There were a million tiny details to take care of:

Who's picking up the cake?
How do we get the rental china in the car without breaking it?
Did everyone get their tuxedo?

Who's bringing the flowers?!

As we scrambled to tie up those last-minute details, I found myself with a knot in my stomach and my last nerve hanging by a thread.

Would everything go off without a hitch?

I'm sure we're not the only ones who've ever found themselves caught ill-prepared. But even though that morning proved to be a mad dash, I still found little moments throughout the day to retrace the steps that had brought us to this place.

Loving Reflections

In my mind's eye, I could see how the seeds of this day had been planted long ago – even as far back as her childhood.

By the time she was five or so, you could already tell she was beginning to recognize the importance of commitment – simply by watching us live out our marriage each day.

Kids aren't dumb. They catch on early and learn so much by example.

And the example we tried to set was this:
Commitment is of the utmost importance.

I realized she had learned to look for a tenderhearted man when, at just seven years old, she witnessed her father say, *"Please forgive me for losing my temper and wrongly accusing you"*.

From that moment – and from that mistake – I concluded that being a hard-nose all the time didn't necessarily teach her what a real man was all about.

Or at eight, when she asked, *"Why am I in your wedding video?"* and mom explained, *"Anyone can be a father, but it takes someone special to be a daddy."*

After hearing that, she climbed into my lap, hugged my neck, and said, *"You're mine and Mom's hero."*

I think that was the bonding moment when I truly knew I had become her **Daddy.**

As the day progressed, my thoughts turned to her adolescence.

My family is no different than anyone else's, and I can recall a few rough patches when guiding her wasn't so easy.

Sometimes we wondered if she would ever make it through puberty unscathed.

But we knew – without question – that leaving her to figure out sex on her own was **not** an option.

From those early years, we made it a point that anything was open for discussion. Because nothing was considered taboo, she always came to us for a straight answer – no matter how shocking the question might have been.

Still, I worried whether she had made the right choice for her life.

But the more I thought about it, the more convinced I became – **yes, she did.**

Most importantly, she had not attached herself physically, and that allowed her to use wisdom in choosing a mate.

I would occasionally hear her sizing up potential boyfriends using that 1 Corinthians 13 passage. I'd hear her say:
"Well, this guy wasn't too kind, was he?"
"He's not a very patient person."
All the right questions – the ones that needed answering – she had the chance to ask *before it was too late.*

My fears began to subside as I checked off the last item on my to-do list, jumped back in my car, and headed north toward the wedding.

The Moment Had Arrived

With less than two hours to go, I approached the circle drive that led into the Chateaux – an event center with a 20-foot crystal chandelier, a two-story bay window, polished wood floors, and ivy-laced balconies.

It was the perfect backdrop for a once-in-a-lifetime occasion, and already the flood of family and friends had begun to arrive.

The night was charged with so much excitement, you could almost slice it with a knife.

The clinking of china. The chatter of small talk. The frantic pace of the caterers hustling from one table to another – it was just what we had always envisioned for our little girl's wedding.

As I stood overlooking the commotion from my balcony view just above the dance floor, I took a moment to simply give thanks.

With tears coursing down my cheeks, I thought about how beautiful this wedding had turned out to be. But it wasn't just the atmosphere that got me all choked up – it was the fact that I knew they would be entering their marriage **baggage-free.**

And *that* was the true beauty of it.

The clock was ticking away the last five minutes until the ceremony was to begin, and the knot in my stomach suddenly grew larger.

Standing at the top of the winding staircase, I turned and looked into my daughter's face – and I'll never forget what I saw.

She was aglow – radiant with the kind of innocence only sexual purity can bring.

She turned and smiled at me, and I knew right then and there: **we had done something right.**

That moment froze in time.

That smile wasn't just the joy of a bride on her wedding day – it was the silent conversation between a father and his daughter.

A moment that said, "*Thank you for fighting for me.*"

All the years of struggle…all the prayers whispered in the dark…all the fears that we might have failed her – they were answered in that single look.

It was a silent benediction over a journey that was well-traveled.
We had broken the cycle that haunted our families, and we had done it **through our own child.**

Those five minutes flew by like five seconds as the music began to play.

Descending the staircase to her awaiting groom, my eye caught his, and I thought about how this young man was everything we had discussed that night in the restaurant.

He was patient. He was kind. He wasn't boastful or proud. And most importantly, he was a man willing to prove the sincerity of his love *by his actions.*

It would be a privilege for me to give my daughter's hand to a man of that character.

And that's exactly what I did when the minister asked, *"Who gives this woman to be this man's lawfully wedded wife?"*

I spoke out with conviction,
"Her mother and I do,"

And I meant every word of it.

Those tears that my wife and I shed that night weren't tears of sorrow.
Oh sure, we were going to miss her – but this wedding was more than a ceremony.

It was a **celebration** of how their commitment to purity had come full circle.

For us, it was an honor.

We knew this was God's design for marriage – a life unshackled by baggage.

Facing each other, with the two-story window behind them, they exchanged their lifelong vows – and we knew they weren't just reciting empty words.

They hadn't let themselves get so wrapped up in one another that they overlooked the flaws. Instead, they made it a priority to enter marriage with **eyes wide open** – and that's exactly what they did.

"For better or for worse, for richer or poorer, in sickness and in health, and forsaking all others..."

The rings exchanged. The blessing was pronounced.

And then, as a way to commemorate their commitment to purity – they shared a small box of chocolates together.

Words can't fully express the joy and pride we felt that evening.

Now that I've seen this firsthand, I'm confident we can change the mindset of a generation.

Being different seems to be programmed into the genetic makeup of every teenager.

So let's place before them the challenge of being different **– by being a virgin.**

Maybe it will turn out to be the norm…and not just the exception.

A pure and innocent wedding didn't happen *to* us – but we made it happen *for* our daughter.

And by doing so, we've found ourselves experiencing a massive new beginning.

You can do this for your kids too –

and there's **NO EXPERIENCE NECESSARY!**

Epilogue

This book was never meant to hurt those who feel they've failed in the past.

Its purpose is to inspire **life-change** – for you, and for all those who follow.

And no one is more deserving of that change than **you**.

When this book was first written, we had been married for about 20 years.

Today, we're celebrating **41** – and still going strong!

Our daughter and her husband have now been married **23 years**, and just last year, we had the joy of witnessing one of their daughters get married.

Three generations of change – two of them with a baggage-free beginning.

Now, I understand that not every family looks the same. Yours may or may not fit the traditional mother/father scenario.

Each family is unique, with its own dynamics and challenges.

But regardless of your situation, the ideas in this book are **invaluable** to any parent who cares deeply about their child's future.

No book – this one included – can replace what a small act of parental involvement can accomplish.

You may be a single parent, but that doesn't mean you can't make a powerful impact.
Or maybe you've been distant, and are only now realizing how important your role is – this can be your wakeup call.

And if both parents are involved – even if separated – that's a step in the right direction.

But let's be honest:
If you're constantly tearing down your ex-spouse, you're not helping your child.

That's still their mom or dad – someone your child still loves, whether **you** do or not.

Wherever you are on the parenting spectrum, it's **never too late** to jump in and make a change.

But understand this: years of neglect won't be repaired in an instant. It takes **time**.

Maybe you're wondering:
How can I model a cherishing marriage when I've already destroyed it?

My advice is simple: **ask for forgiveness.**
Not just from your spouse – but from your child, too.

You don't need to cower, but it takes a strong man or woman to humble themselves and admit they were wrong.

Few things are more powerful than **genuine repentance.**

Your child needs to see that you have the integrity to own your mistakes – and that you're
willing to grow from them.

When they do, their respect for you will grow deeper.

Can you reconnect with your child **this late in the game**?

Yes, you can.

And it starts with one simple four-letter word:
Time.

"Whoever said, 'Quality over quantity,' never raised teenagers."

Often, "quality time" ends up being a once-a-year vacation. But you'd be surprised at how much your teens remember from everyday conversations and ordinary family moments.

So if you've failed to spend time until now – **start today**.

Sit down with your child and ask for their forgiveness. You might be amazed – kids are far more forgiving than we expect, especially when they see **real sincerity**.

While we've talked a lot about teaching your kids purity, I'd be remiss if I didn't tell you the real key to this book: The truth of the **Gospel of Christ**.
Every idea shared in these pages works best when it's em-

powered by one thing – your personal relationship with **Jesus Christ**.

So, I encourage you to examine your heart.

If your relationship with Him isn't what it should be, there's no better time than now to make a change.

If you haven't been the example God has called you to be, I'd be honored to lead you in a prayer of repentance.

If that's your desire, pray this with me:

> **Lord, I haven't been the parent my children need. Please help me show them the example of a broken man or woman who has placed their insufficiencies in the hands of an all-sufficient God. Please forgive me for my failures and help me overcome the sin that has ruled my life. I place my trust in the one and only true God – Jesus of Nazareth. Amen.**

Parents, I hope you'll take this book to heart and **run with it**.

Your kids deserve the best life has to offer - **help them find it!**

Addendum

The Male Version

In Chapter 4, I alluded to a male version of the 1 Corinthians 13 talk, as well as the Chocolate Box Illustration.

Here is my take on how that can be accomplished.

Around his thirteenth birthday, I planned a father-and-son guys' night out.
I walked through the same general scenario I had previously shared with my daughter—but this time, the adaptation was a little different.

The Test
Using the same 1 Corinthians 13 scripture as my foundation, I began.

However, instead of choosing "Johnny" as the protagonist, I refocused the story on **respect** and placed my son as the central character.

I told him,
"Words can be cheap. But if you really love her the way you say you do, the proof of that love will show in your actions toward her."

I then read the familiar passage:
"Love is patient, love is kind. It does not envy... Love never fails." (1 Corinthians 13:4–8)
I continued,
"I believe God is the author of true love—and the way true love is expressed is through the design He created."
"If you want to know whether you measure up to God's expectations, test yourself."

"When you're with a girl, ask yourself..."

- Am I patient with her—respecting her body as a gift from God?
- Do I brag to my friends about what I think I can get away with when we're alone?

- Am I too proud to say we're saving ourselves for marriage?

- Do I have self-control, or do I let my desires push her into something she's not ready for?

- Am I pursuing my own satisfaction...or honoring the truth of what God designed for marriage?"

Then I asked him,

"Do you pass this test of love?"

Like I said — words can be cheap. But your actions? Your actions are the true proof of sincerity."

The Illustration

As before, I continued:

"Someday you'll meet the right person, ask for her hand in marriage, and follow through on that commitment."

*"But until that happens, God has given you an incredibly important gift—the gift of **purity**."*

"I know that, as a man, the word purity might sound weak or unmanly today. But it's not.

It's a strong character trait—and one that's becoming increasingly rare.

"At that point, I reached into my pocket and pulled out a small box of chocolates—the kind with just four pieces in the package—and began the illustration.

I placed the elegantly wrapped box on the table like a wedding gift and said,

"This represents your purity. It's a gift that can only be given once—and only to one person.
God intended it to be shared with your lifelong mate."

"This gift was meant for your future wife. It was never intended to be spread around to multiple others. I know your mom always taught you to share – but in this case, that's not what she meant".

"So, let's say one day you decide to experiment with your gift early. You're alone with someone and take advantage of the situation—compromising your purity."

"Maybe you touch her inappropriately. Even if it doesn't go all the way, this once-untouched gift has now been tampered with. And not just yours – but hers as well".

I then removed the bow from the package, keeping the box in full view.

"As time goes on, another dating opportunity comes along. You push the limits a little farther, pressuring your date to go past her comfort zone. You follow through with using her for your pleasure."

"Even if the gift is still technically intact, you're now feeling guilt and regret."

At that point, I began tearing the wrapping paper off the box.

"You didn't get what you came for – so you move on to the next."

"Still on your quest, you meet someone new. You pressure her to prove her devotion—and she reluctantly caves. You both give your gifts away."

I opened the box, removed two pieces of chocolate and placed them on the table.

"Now, when you look back at your gift of purity, what's left to share with your wife?"
I held up the torn, tattered, half-empty box.

Then I reached into my pocket again and pulled out a second, identical box—**perfectly intact**. I placed them side by side.

"Which gift do you want to offer your wife on your honeymoon night?"

Do you want to give her a fresh, untouched gift—or a damaged shell of what it was meant to be?"

"Forced passion is not sexually satisfying. It's not about fulfilling a basic urge – it's about building a life-long connection."

"Do you really want someone to feel like a doormat – like they were just used?

Take it from me – you'll want someone who's willing to give themselves freely… and that's what leads to a lasting relationship."

"Honoring her in this way during courtship will result in her being willing to give herself – and her body—wholeheartedly when the time is right."

"Please think about it. And ask yourself: What do I want for my wife – and for my marriage?"

About the Author

Hi, I'm Randal Lee — a graduate of Southwestern Assemblies of God University in Waxahachie, Texas. These days, I call the Northern Front Range of Colorado home.

My wife and I have been married for 41 wonderful years, and God has blessed us with two amazing kids—both married—and ten incredible grandkids. (Yes, you heard that right — ten! It felt like running a daycare at times.)

We currently attend an Assemblies of God church in Fort Morgan, Colorado. In the past, our ministry has centered on doing what we love most: encouraging families, both here in Colorado and throughout the Dallas Metroplex of Texas. Our heart is to help parents guide their children toward strong, healthy marriages and a deeper walk with God.

That's really what this book is all about. *Teaching Purity in an Unpure World* was written out of our passion to help others walk a better path — even when the culture around us says otherwise. We look forward to sharing this message with today's generation.

If you'd like to connect — or if you're interested in having me speak at your event — I'd love to hear from you. You can reach me at: **randal@purityrules.com**

Acknowledgements

To my wife, "Kaffy" (my nickname for her), for all of her love, commitment, and dedication. You are God's gift to me on this journey. I love you and always will.

To my children, for being blessings I don't deserve and for giving your mother and me the joy of being grandparents — to ten of the most special young people we could have ever asked for.

To our friends and family, who have helped us see this project through to completion.

To Pastors Chuck and Chris Griffin, who have supported us through prayer and timely words of wisdom, and who have ministered to us through the Word of God. It is an honor to be under your leadership.

And most of all,

To my Father and Lord, JESUS CHRIST, who planted this idea in my heart so many years ago. He has proven Himself faithful and has provided both the finances and the vision to complete the task He placed before me. He deserves *all* the credit.

References

All scripture quotes are from the New International Version. The NIV/KVJ Parallel Bible Copyright ©1985 All rights reserved. Scriptures taken from the HOLY BIBLE, NEW INTERNATIONAL VERSION Copyright © 1973, 1974, 1984, International Bible Society. Used by permission of Zondervan Bible Publishers.

Except where noted: ™
The Message Bible (The Bible in Contemporary Language.) Nav Press, Colorado Springs, CO. Scripture taken from THE MESSAGE copyright © 1993, 1994, 1995, 1996, 2000, 2001, 2002. Used by permission of NavPress Publishing Group.